Citizenship

Being Responsible

Cassie Mayer

Heinemann Library
Chicago, Illinois

Customer Service 888-454-2279
Visit our website at www.heinemannraintree.com

Designed by Joanna Hinton-Malivoire
Illustrated by Mark Beech
Printed and bound in China by South China Printing Co. Ltd.

11 10 09 08 07
10 9 8 7 6 5 4 3 2 1

The Library of Congress has cataloged the first edition of this book as follows:
Mayer, Cassie.
  Being responsible / Cassie Mayer.
       p. cm. -- (Citizenship)
  Includes bibliographical references and index.
  ISBN 978-1-4034-9489-4 (hc) -- ISBN 978-1-4034-9497-9 (pbk.) 1. Responsibility--Juvenile literature. I. Title.
  BJ1451.M39 2007
  179'.9--dc22
                              2006039382

Contents

Being responsible means you do
the right thing.

Being responsible means taking
charge of what you do.

When you clean your room
without being asked to ...

you are being responsible.

When you put on your seat belt
without being asked to ...

you are being responsible.

When you feed your pet without being asked to ...

you are being responsible.

When you look after your brother without being asked to ...

you are being responsible.

When you throw away trash
without being asked to ...

14

you are being responsible.

When you brush your teeth
without being asked to ...

you are being responsible.

When you admit to a mistake ...

you are being responsible.

It is important to be responsible.

How can you be responsible?

Activity

How is this child being responsible?

Picture Glossary

admit tell something that you may be afraid to tell

responsible able to be trusted; taking care of yourself, your chores, and the people around you

Index

Note to Parents and Teachers
Each book in this series shows examples of behavior that demonstrate good citizenship. Take time to discuss each illustration and ask children to identify the responsible behavior shown. Use the question on page 21 to ask students how they can be responsible in their own lives.

The text has been chosen with the advice of a literacy expert to enable beginning readers success while reading independently or with moderate support. You can support children's nonfiction literacy skills by helping them use the table of contents, picture glossary, and index.

302   Mayer, Cassie.
Ma   Being responsible .
          37085100137353

DATE			